Some Days You Might As Well Laugh

Sayings and Thoughts to Help You
Keep a Sense of Humor

Inspired by Faith

Some Days You Might As Well Laugh
ISBN 978-0-9848369-0-1

Published by Product Concept Mfg., Inc.
2175 N. Academy Circle #200, Colorado Springs, CO 80909

©2011 Product Concept Mfg., Inc. All rights reserved.

Sayings not having a credit listed are contributed by writers
for Product Concept Mfg., Inc. or in a rare case,
the author is unknown.

Written and Compiled by Patricia Mitchell
in association with Product Concept Mfg., Inc.

There's nothing better than laughter
to smooth out the potholes of life!

Life is a bumpy ride— don't we know it! But for those of us who can look on the light side, a lot of those potholes look less like craters and more like simple dips in the road. With its ageless ability to lift a mood, lighten a heart, and refresh a downcast spirit, laughter is the surest route to a joyful journey.

This collection of cartoons, quips, and quotes is designed to relax you, entertain you, and offer you another way of looking at things. Some may bring a smile, and some may make you laugh out loud. A few will stick with you long after you have chuckled in recognition and agreement. These are the road-smoothers, the gentle cushions, the sweet blessings that carry you over the rough spots. These are the supporters and encouragers that keep you going and keep you smiling.

Let these pages bring out the grins. Enjoy a section at a time, or simply flip open the book and start reading. Perhaps you'd like to pick an apt one-liner as a theme for your day, and possibly share it with someone else who could use a chuckle (and who couldn't?). Consider placing a little "laugh note" on the mirror, or tuck it in your wallet, or leave it on a coworker's chair. Laughter is the best blessing this side of heaven—and the most rewarding one to give away.

Ha, ha, ha!

Some days you just gotta grin and bear it!

If you can laugh at yourself,
you'll never run out of
things to laugh at.

**It's never too late to
have a happy childhood.**

Ruin the day for a grouch:
smile!

**Imagination was given to man
to compensate him for what he
is not; a sense of humor
to console him for what he is.**

-Francis Bacon

For instant relief, try laughter!

Every cloud has a silver lining, as long as it's raining on someone else.

We are all here for a spell; get all the good laughs you can.

-Will Rogers

Don't worry about what's happening today—tomorrow could be worse!

Laugh!
Crying's the only alternative.

A cheerful heart is good medicine.

-Proverbs 17:22 NIV

Even if there's nothing to laugh at,
laugh on credit.

Mix a little foolishness
with your serious plans:
it's lovely to be silly
at the right moment.

-Horace

Happiness consists of living
each day as if it were
the first day of your honeymoon
and the last day of your vacation.

I start every day with a smile—
that way, I get it over with.

When people can laugh together,
they usually can get along together.

*A little levity will save many
a good heavy thing from sinking.*

-Samuel Butler

Keep smiling—it makes people
wonder what you've been up to.

*Laugh and the world laughs
with you. Cry and you streak
your mascara.*

A joke that has to be explained
is at its wit's end.

**Even if you could buy happiness,
some people would
try to bargain.**

Nothing like a little judicious levity.

-Robert Louis Stevenson

**Laughter might not make
things better, but it will
make you happier.**

Laugh now. These are the
"good old days" you're going
to fondly remember later.

*Show me someone who lets a
smile be his umbrella,
and I'll show you someone
with a mouthful of rain!*

If you can enjoy the scenery on the
detour, you're not lost!

Ever wonder how much deeper the ocean would be without sponges?

If you didn't laugh at the last joke you heard, you probably didn't hear it from your boss.

All nature wears one universal grin.

-Henry Fielding

Laughter is like changing a baby's diaper—it doesn't permanently solve any problems, but it makes things more pleasant for a while.

If you doubt God has a sense of humor, you've never seen a duck-billed platypus.

Things always look brighter
through a smile.

*Sure, you can catch more flies
with honey than with vinegar;
but who wants to catch flies?*

Most folks are about as happy
as they make up their minds to be.

-Abraham Lincoln

*Used to be we'd sit down
to dinner and count our blessings
instead of our calories.*

A day without sunshine—is night.

*I may as well laugh
at my problems—
after all,
everyone else does.*

If you want to make
headlines tomorrow,
try sleeping on a
corduroy pillow tonight.

*If you want to hear God laugh,
just tell Him your plans!*

Getting Along

If it weren't for everybody else, we'd be fine!

It's true that children
brighten a home—
they never turn off any lights!

*A friend not in need
is a friend indeed.*

My teenager accuses me of being
too nosy. At least that's what she
keeps putting in her diary.

*Show me a twin birth,
and I'll show you
an infant replay.*

There's not a family tree in the world
without a few nuts in it.

*Answers are what we have
for other people's problems.*

Our baby has started eating solids—
his crib, the rocker, the coffee table.

*New parents are people
who carry baby photos
where dollars used to be.*

Thank God for your parents—
Adam and Eve never had any!

Inhibited people
are all tied up in "nots"!

If you do housework for $200 a
week, you have a business; if you do
it for free, you have a husband.

A family is a group
of people, who each like a
different breakfast cereal.

I told my husband
to change the baby, and he brought
home a different kid.

*It's sad when your twin sister
forgets your birthday.*

If you want to hear from long-lost
relatives, simply rent a cottage at the
beach for the summer.

*Nowadays, three-year-olds have
all the questions and 13-year-
olds have all the answers.*

An allowance is what you pay your
kids to live with you.

Wrinkles are hereditary—
you get them from your children.

If you can't give thanks
for the relatives you have,
at least give thanks
for the ones you don't.

The best gift for the
relative who has everything
is a burglar alarm.

Two antennas decided
to get married.
The wedding was just so-so,
but the reception
was outstanding!

**Wealth is relative—
the more wealth,
the more relatives.**

Keep your eyes wide open before
marriage, half shut afterwards.

-Benjamin Franklin

**The thing your kids outgrow first
is your wallet.**

God gives us our relatives—thank God we can choose our friends.

-Ethel Watts Mumford

The melon and the honeydew are planning a lavish wedding because they cantaloupe.

Your real friends see you making a fool of yourself and do not think that the condition is permanent.

Some people bring blessings wherever they go; others, whenever they go.

Mrs. Bigger had a baby
bigger than she was,
because he was a little Bigger.

**A parent is a banker
provided by nature.**

Any married man should
forget his mistakes; there's no use
in two people remembering
the same thing.

**Providence protects children
and idiots. I know, because I
have tested it.**

-Mark Twain

If being a mother were easy,
fathers would be doing it.

**Blessed are the flexible, for they
will not get bent out of shape.**

An infant is nature's way of showing
you what your house looks like at
2 o'clock in the morning.

**Learn from the mistakes of
others—you don't have enough
time to make them all yourself.**

By the time we realize our parents
were right, we've got kids
who tell us we're wrong.

If your social network crashed,
how would you know
who your friends are?

Lots of us are good at giving advice,
but finding someone interested
in receiving it is another matter.

Nothing wrong with my
kid's appetite—
his favorite food is seconds!

If youth had wisdom, kids would
sure miss out on a lot of fun.

Got an attitude?

Just tellin' it like it is...

I don't have pet peeves. I've got a whole kennel full of annoyances.

If I don't go out and do something completely crazy, I'll go nuts!

I'll take advice, as long as it doesn't interfere with what I plan to do.

I know I should stop procrastinating, and someday I might get around to it.

There is nothing so absurd
or ridiculous that has not
at some time been said by
some philosopher.

-Oliver Goldsmith

**How about this—
I'll admit I'm right
if you'll admit you're wrong.**

I don't like people who keep talking
when I'm trying to interrupt.

**Once I thought I was wrong,
but I was mistaken.**

Of course, you're unique
just like everyone else!

**Ever stop to think
and then forget to start again?**

I'm very humble,
and very proud of it, too!

**If at first you don't succeed,
skydiving is not for you.**

It's true that I'm always wishing for something I don't have—but really, what else is there to wish for?

Be sincere—
even if you don't mean it.

There's one thing I admire about egotists—they never talk about other people!

Any idiot can face a crisis;
it is this day-to-day living
that wears you out.

-Anton Chekhov

Life would be so much easier
if only it had subtitles.

**Don't spend all your time looking
for the softest thing in life—you
just might find it under your hat.**

If someone tells you he's laying all
his cards on the table, count 'em.

**I tolerate other people's views—
after all, everyone's entitled
to be wrong.**

Am I ambivalent? Well, yes and no.

*It's hard for me
to make a comeback,
because I haven't been
anywhere in the first place.*

I don't know if I'm apathetic or not,
and I don't care, either.

*Just when I thought
I was getting the picture,
someone changed the scene.*

Of all the things I've lost,
I miss my mind the most.

*My opinion may shift
from time to time,
but never the conviction
that I'm right.*

As I said before,
I never repeat myself.

I used to have a handle on life,
and then it broke.

*People just don't want
to take responsibility
for anything anymore—
but don't quote me on that.*

I have no problem loving my
enemies. It drives them crazy!

Yes, I've had a nice day,
but I have to scream now.

The trouble with life is that
there's no background music
to let me know what's coming.

People who think they know it all
really annoy those of us who do.

My tongue may weigh
next to nothing, but I sure have
a lot of trouble holding it!

Worry works like a charm—
99% of the stuff I worry about
never happens!

With my luck,
the light at the end of the tunnel
is an oncoming train.

It's OK to take my advice,
because I'm not using it.

There's nothing more annoying than someone who thinks he knows everything—and does.

I can keep a secret. It's those people I tell it to who can't keep their mouths shut.

Don't let stress get you down— remember, Moses started out as a basket case!

I try to make everyone's day a little more surreal.

I'd like to have more self-esteem,
but I don't deserve it.

If you think no one is listening,
you might be right—
until you say something stupid.

Behind my crabby exterior
lies an even crabbier interior.

It's true that God provides
the birds with food, but He doesn't
throw it into their nest.

*I don't believe anything
until it's been officially denied.*

Truth is stranger than fiction,
but not nearly as popular.

Looking Good!

Smile - it's like a free facelift!

On-line gym membership is great—
I can go without ever leaving the house!

I took up swimming at 60
so no one would know
whether I've got wrinkles,
or I stayed in the water too long.

Beautiful young people are works of nature; but beautiful old people are works of art.

To lose weight, you need to give up only two things—a knife and a fork.

Those who don't lie about their age either are too young to have anything to lose, or too old to have anything to gain.

The best thing about
the current trend in fashion
is that it won't last long.

It's true, your mirror never lies;
but at least it's not laughing.

Midlife starts ten years out
from wherever you are now.

If swimming is such good
exercise, why aren't
whales skinny?

I'd put my hair back to its
natural color if only I could
remember what it is.

*A bathroom scale is something
you step on, and then scream at.*

I don't eat it if the list of ingredients
takes up more than half the package.

*The dietician told me
to eat more greens.
"Be like a rabbit!" she said.
So I did, but now
I'm tripping over my ears!*

The best way to buy jeans
is with hindsight.

*You can tell how healthy you are
by what you take two at a time—
stairs or pills.*

Why is it, after spending an hour
doing aerobics, we get mad if we
can't find the remote control?

*The great advantage of being
bald is that you can style your
hair with a damp cloth!*

There's an easy way to avoid wrinkles: unscrew the light bulb next to the bathroom mirror.

I have so much gold in my teeth that I sleep with my head in a safe!

At the department store counter, I asked for a jar of wrinkle cream. Once I was through with the transaction, my little daughter looked up at me and said, "Wow, Mom, you really spend a lot to have so many wrinkles!"

You can't depend on age to bring wisdom, but it guarantees gray hair.

I hate calories because they always
hit below the belt.

**Wrinkles should merely indicate
where smiles have been.**

-Mark Twain

Old age is when you find yourself
using one bend-over
to pick up two things.

**A hair on the head
is worth two on the brush.**

If God wanted me to touch my toes,
He would have put them
up around my waist!

By the time we start learning
to watch our step,
we're not stepping out anymore.

The best vitamin for a Christian is B1.

Beauty always comes
from within—
bottles, tubes, jars, spritzers.

Blessed are they
who hunger and thirst,
for they are sticking
to their diets.

*Ever since I put grease
on my hair, everything keeps
slipping my mind.*

How come a one-pound
box of candy makes you
put on an extra five?

*Time may heal,
but it sure doesn't beautify.*

Youth is when you think you'll live forever. Old age is when you wonder how you've lived so long.

At a certain age, yesterday's dimple becomes today's wrinkle.

At a certain age, everything starts to click; beginning with your knees, then your hips, then your elbows.

If God wanted me to be thin, then why did He make food taste so good?

People think I get a lot of exercise—
they always tell me I'm jumping
to conclusions.

The only thing between me
and baldness is my hair.

We do not stop playing
because we grow old;
we grow old because
we stop playing.

As teens, we use make-up to look older. In middle age, we use it to look younger; and beyond that, we use it to look presentable.

**It's a sure sign
that you're over the hill
if you're too tired to climb it.**

You know you've reached middle age when you dim the lights for economic reasons, not romantic ones.

Eat, drink, and be merry,
for tomorrow we diet.

*I believe that having a good
breakfast will keep you from
getting hungry all day. I believe
that until around lunchtime.*

I'm on a seafood diet—
every time I see food, I eat it!

If you cheat on your diet,
you'll gain in the end.

**My idea of good exercise
is to shop faster.**

Why would anyone go to
the gym for a stair-stepping class,
then go to work and
take the elevator?

The only thing about a double-fudge banana split that can make you gain weight is the spoon you dip into it.

Sure, two can live a cheaply as one—if one doesn't eat, that is!

My favorite machine at the gym is the vending machine.

Amen!

Heavenly humor brings saintly smiles!

*There are four classes
of church members:
the tired, the retired, the tireless,
and the tiresome.*

The naughtiest person in the Bible has to be Moses—he broke all ten commandments at once!

Adam was so lucky—every joke he told had never been told before.

Our new pastor is from Germany— we call him our German Shepherd!

Lots of people want to serve God, but only in an advisory capacity.

Did you hear the joke
about the church bell?
It's never been tolled.

*If absence makes
the heart grow fonder,
people must really
love our church.*

There's no prerequisite
for being a Christian—
you learn it on the job.

Constantly harping on something
does not make you an angel.

**The defects in a preacher
are soon spied.**

-Martin Luther

Isn't it funny how people want to be
at the front of the bus,
the back of the church,
and in the middle of the road?

A church janitor needs to mind
his keys and pews.

**A church committee
is a group that keeps minutes
but loses hours.**

There will be prayer
in public schools as long as
there are algebra tests.

**Noah is known as the organizer
of the first couples' cruise.**

God loves everyone,
but probably favors "fruits of the
Spirit" over religious nuts.

**If God is your co-pilot,
swap seats immediately!**

The road to heaven starts
at the narrow way.

You have to get to church
pretty early on Sunday morning
to get a seat in the back row.

**To prevent truth decay,
brush up on the Bible!**

Church is a place where you meet
nodding acquaintances.

**God created man and woman,
and then He started
getting complaints.**

God was able to create the world in six days because He wasn't working with a committee.

Some Christians are more familiar with the 23rd Psalm than they are the Shepherd.

Cleanliness may be next to godliness, but with toddlers, it's next to impossible.

The distance between Earth and Heaven is not a matter of altitude, but of attitude.

The house of many mansions
requires reservations in advance.

You have to understand—the Ten
Commandments didn't come with
a multiple choice option.

Some people treat religion like a
spare tire—they don't bring it out
unless there's an emergency.

Every Christmas someone says
it's the best one ever.
I always thought the
first one was.

It wasn't the apple on the tree that did so much damage—it was the pair on the ground!

Those who kneel before God can stand before anyone.

Nothing else ruins the truth like stretching it.

Forbidden fruits create many jams.

Sometimes God puts us in the dark so we'll finally see the light.

Time for a Check-up

A laugh a day keeps the doctor away!

I was delighted with my group medical insurance until I got sick. Then they told me I couldn't collect on it until the group got sick.

There's a new drug on the market.
It's half aspirin and half glue for
people who get splitting headaches.

**Don't fight a cold—
that's what makes a cold sore.**

I'm beginning to wonder
about my physician—
all her patients seem to be sick.

**After getting the bill
for my surgery, I understand
why doctors wear masks
in the operating room.**

How come I weigh ten pounds more
on the scale at the doctor's office
than I do on the scale at home?

A good doctor
can add ten years to your life—
just sitting in the waiting room.

My dentist gave me some
bad news today—my teeth are fine,
but my gums need to come out.

The person most often late
for a doctor's appointment
is the doctor.

Lots of products say
they're good for aches and pains.
But who wants aches and pains?

The only way to keep your health
is to eat what you don't want,
drink what you don't like,
and do what you'd rather not.

-Mark Twain

A minor operation
is one performed on someone else.

You'll be released from the
hospital as soon as they think
you're well enough to see the bill.

The one thing the doctor
liked about my test results
was that they weren't hers.

*God does the healing,
and the doctor sends the bill.*

One time
I sat in the waiting room so long
that I recovered.

My doctor gave me a guaranteed
cure for insomnia: sleep.

**My surgeon left his sponge in me.
It's not a problem,
except I get really thirsty.**

Never go to a clinic where
hypodermic needles are
stored on a dartboard.

**My physician told me to take
a hot bath before retiring.
That's ridiculous—I'm decades
away from retiring!**

My physician advised me to turn
my body over to someone
who will exercise it.

I told my doctor I had shingles,
and he tried to sell
me aluminum siding.

The best doctors in the world are
Dr. Diet, Dr. Quiet,
and Dr. Merryman.

-Jonathan Swift

In an attempt to cut costs,
Main St. Hospital installed
do-it-yourself operating tables.

I wish I had a dental appointment to cancel—it really brightens my day!

A hypochondriac is someone who can't leave being well-enough alone.

My doctor said I could stop the stabbing pain in my eye, that happens when I drink coffee, by taking the stirring stick out of the cup first.

I think I'd make a wonderful doctor—after all, people tell me I've got the handwriting for it.

I asked my doctor for a second opinion, so he billed me twice.

My pharmacist told me to take one tablet every four hours, or as often as I could get the cap off the bottle.

A wolf in sheep's clothing needs professional help.

My physician says I've got many good years left, as long as I exercise, eat healthy, and stay away from natural causes.

My doctor diagnosed me with a hereditary condition, so I asked him to send the bill to my dad.

I was expelled from medical school because they could read my handwriting.

If four out of five people suffer from headaches, does that mean one person enjoys them?

An apple a day keeps the doctor away, but a clove of garlic a day keeps everyone away!

Be careful about reading health books. You may die of a misprint.

-Mark Twain

If your soul is healthy, all the rest is secondary.

Business as Usual

The best thing to wear to work is a smile.

Women have a harder time making it to the top than men—they don't have wives to help them get there.

I don't mind being average. It simply means I'm as close to the top as I am to the bottom.

My computer gets more work done than I do because it doesn't have to attend staff meetings.

I never drink coffee at my desk. It keeps me awake all day.

Brilliant employees invent,
smart ones do,
and I like to sit and watch them.

*I was gung-ho
to climb the ladder of success,
but now I'd be satisfied
with a low footstool.*

Your friends will always cheer
your successes—
as long as your successes
don't top their own.

There's no point in getting
to work early. No one's there
to praise you for it.

If a cluttered desk means a
cluttered mind, then what's an
empty desk mean?

Wishful thinking convinces us
we can run the business
better than the boss.

Income is something it's hard
to live without,
but even harder to live within.

The worst day to get sick
is on your day off.

*I'm so used to stress at work
that when I don't feel any,
I get nervous.*

You have your doubts
when the boss says:

a. This will be a short meeting.

b. Your request is under
consideration.

c. This project won't take much
of your time.

d. Don't worry, the overtime
requirement is only temporary.

e. We're in the process of taking
care of that.

The sooner you let your work
get behind, the longer you'll have
to catch up.

**If it weren't for the
last minute, nothing would get
done around here.**

When you start looking
like your passport photo,
it's time to ask for time off.

**To beat the 5 o'clock rush,
leave work at noon.**

I've got the perfect way
to handle office emails—
it's called the delete key.

*I love my work! Why, I could sit
and look at it all day.*

I get lots of exercise
dodging deadlines.

*The boss called a meeting
to announce that the office was
going paperless. Then he gave
each of us a ten-page hand-out
telling us how.*

The project ahead of you
is small potatoes compared to
the Power behind you.

I used to work
in a muffler factory,
but I quit when I got exhausted.

My boss always calls staff
meetings at 4 o'clock on Friday. That
way, he can invite questions without
worrying that somebody
will actually ask one.

A committee is a group of people
who individually can do nothing,
but as a committee,
decide that nothing can be done.

**In any office, after all is said and
done, more is said than done.**

If you want your coworkers to think
you know more than they do,
walk fast and look worried.

**Even if hard work won't kill me,
I can't see taking the chance.**

Accomplish the impossible,
and your boss will add it
to your job description.

*My boss said he made a mental
note to raise my pay, but I think
he wrote it in disappearing ink.*

If it weren't for the office,
where would we go to rest up
after vacation?

*Life is what you make it,
which could explain what I read
on a lot of resumes.*

When I'm not in my right mind,
my left mind gets really overworked.

**Never put off until tomorrow
what you can avoid altogether.**

My company's dental plan is
"chew on the other side."

**Plan ahead—it wasn't raining
when Noah built the ark.**

If at first you don't succeed,
then redefine success.

**If at first you do succeed,
try not to look shocked.**

I began to worry about our new CEO
when he asked me how often the
company's annual report came out.

**My company reached the
ultimate in cost cutbacks—
it went out of business.**

It's Only Money

Thank goodness, smiles are free!

The surest way to remain poor
is to pretend you are rich.

For your tithe,
give God what's right—
not what's left.

There are many more important
things in life than money,
but most of them cost money.

All you can do on a shoestring
anymore is trip over it.

*I don't know how much money
I have in the bank.
I haven't shaken it lately.*

Whoever said
money can't buy happiness
sure didn't know where to shop!

*Some people pay their bills
when due, some when overdue,
and some never do.*

I got burned in the stock market
after I picked up a hot tip.

*A fool and his money
are soon parted, but what makes
me wonder is how they got
together in the first place.*

I used to think I could save the world.
Now I'm finding it hard
to save a little money.

*If they ever run an experiment
on the effect of sudden wealth,
count me in!*

The holy passion of friendship
is of so sweet and steady and loyal
and enduring a nature that it will
last through a whole lifetime,
if not asked to lend money.

-Mark Twain

*It used to be that only death
and taxes were inevitable. Now
there's shipping and handling.*

In department stores,
I'm magnetic—
everything I pick up, I charge!

*By the time we've got the money,
we haven't got the time.*

The most expensive vehicle to drive
is a shopping cart.

*Those who despise money
are those who sponge off
their friends.*

History repeats itself, but each time it
does the price goes up.

*Banks have my two favorite
things—money and holidays!*

God doesn't want shares
of your life—He's asking for
controlling interest.

Noah was a great money manager—he was floating his stock while everyone else was in liquidation.

An optimist is someone who, rather than cry because he cannot pay his bills, is glad he's not one of his creditors.

Travel is educational. You learn where ATM machines are located in different cities throughout the world.

Having money is better than being poor, if only for financial reasons.

We stuck to our budget
until our neighbor pulled
up his driveway in a new car.

*The trouble with our economy
is that there are so many ways
to get into debt, but few ways
to get out of it.*

Despite the cost of living,
it still remains popular.

*It's wise to live within your
income, even if you need
to borrow money to do so.*

A credit card is what you use to buy today what you can't afford tomorrow because you're still paying for what you bought yesterday.

Change is inevitable,
except from a vending machine.

I've been good about saving money for a rainy day, and now I have just about enough to buy an umbrella.

It's easy to meet expenses—
they're everywhere.

My neighbor is so rich that he gets
his exercise by folding his money.

*I consolidated all my bills into
one payment. Now all my bills are
paid except one.*

I have a book that makes
all my spending decisions.
It's called a checkbook.

*I was excited about a trip
to the Bahamas until I realized I
couldn't manage the first part—
a trip to the bank.*

Credit cards are a great way to
spend money you wish you had.

*The only way I'll be able to have
folding money in my wallet
is if they put hinges on nickels.*

I've got enough money to last the
rest of my life if I don't eat anything,
buy anything, or turn anything on.

*For the outcome
of a changed life,
try the income of God's Word.*

Around the House

It's where we live, love... and laugh!

It's true—dryers eat socks.

An antique is a piece of furniture that has gone from the living room to the attic and back to the living room.

Your home is where you can't sit down without seeing something that needs cleaning, repairing, or replacing.

I installed a square bath tub so I wouldn't get rings.

I know it's the end of summer when
the neighbors return my deck chairs.

If the grass is greener on the
other side of the fence,
you don't want to pay
his water bill.

The walls in my apartment building
are so thin that when I tell a joke,
the neighbors laugh.

Of course Noah had lights
on the ark—floodlights!

Housework is something no one
notices until you don't do it.

**Birds of a feather flock together
over my patio furniture.**

How come satellite TV
comes in crystal clear as soon as the
repairman walks in the door?

**In my garden, my tomatoes got
almost as big as my blisters.**

I went out to get some
unfinished furniture,
and I came home with a tree.

**Nowadays, a townhouse costs
more than the town used to.**

Few things have a shorter life span
than a clean garage.

**I'm looking for an appliance
guaranteed to outlast
the box it comes in.**

It's good policy to love your neighbor. He just might have the tools you need to borrow.

Our neighborhoods are as sound as ever—thanks to television, radio, CDs, & MP3 Players.

If you can smile when all else is going wrong, you're probably a plumber working for triple time on Sunday afternoon.

It's time to turn up the heat
when you slip on ice as you
step out of the shower.

*Our house was on the market
for so long that we had to
repaint the For Sale sign.*

The quickest way to find
something you've lost in the house
is to buy a replacement.

If your bathroom
seems small to you,
start retiling the floor.
Before you're finished,
you'll appreciate every inch it isn't!

Give weeds an inch,
and they'll take a yard.

Our brand-new house
is nothing to sneeze at.
The walls couldn't take it.

If you're invited to enter a contest called "The World's Dirtiest House," the dust in your house is noticeable.

A subdivision is where they chop down trees and then name streets after them.

When opportunity knocks at the front door, most of us are out in the back yard hunting for the pot of gold at the end of a rainbow.

If God meant for us to rest
on Sundays, why did He
create weeds?

Law of the basement workshop:
Any tool dropped will roll
into the darkest and
least accessible corner.

How long is a minute?
That depends on which side of the
bathroom door you're on!

Tech Treatment

Can't live with 'em... can't live without 'em!

Wow, it works!

Now if only I could remember what I did.

Things you never
used to worry about:

a. losing your telephone

b. watching your typewriter crash

c. fighting an urge to check friends'
status at 2 a.m.

d. hearing your pants pocket ring in
the middle of a sermon

e. getting tendinitis from clicking the
remote control

f. trying to reach a real person
through an automated
answering service

g. owning appliances smarter
than you are

**_To err is human,
but to really mess things up,
you need a computer._**

TV only insults your intelligence;
a computer makes you doubt you
have any intelligence at all.

**Retirement is when your favorite
piece of software is a pillow.**

You can get a computer
that responds to the sound of your
voice—unlike your kids.

**Failure is not an option—it comes
bundled with the software.**

You can depend on your
computer to make mistakes
quickly and accurately.

A computer you buy will be obsolete
before you get it home.

My computer beat me in chess,
but I came out first
in kick-boxing.

I think tweeting is for the birds!

I'd like to back up my files, but
where's the reverse on my PC?

Sometimes I wish God had created
me with a "scroll back" feature.

A printer consists of three main parts: the case, the jammed paper tray, and the blinking red light.

For a list of ways technology has made life confusing, press 3.

Don't byte off more than you can view.

I've got cable TV, a computer, electronic reader, and smart phone, and still my kids tell me I'm behind the times.

Thank goodness for kids!
At least there's someone
who knows how to use the remote!

*If necessity is the mother
of invention, how come
so many unnecessary things
keep getting invented?*

It used to be that a virus
only made you sick;
now your computer can catch it, too.

I found a gadget that could do half
my work for me, so I bought two.

**Your printer is that thing
next to your desk with a jammed
paper tray and blinking red light.**

The good thing about TV
commercials is that they're never
interrupted for breaking news.

**Computers must be smarter
than people—you never see one
jogging, do you?**

I use my digital computer all the time—when I run out of fingers, I go on to my toes.

I had to buy a new computer because I couldn't teach my old mouse new clicks.

A picture is worth a thousand words, but it uses up three thousand times the memory.

The techie says he'll get the bugs ironed out for me, but I have to wonder how flat bugs will make my PC run faster.

Computer games are good
at keeping our minds off our minds.

*I love cable TV! I get to see all
those old movies that I walked
out on 20 years ago!*

Stay open to new ideas. Why, the
guy who invented spray paint got
the idea when he sneezed with his
mouth full of tomato juice.

Got Wheels?

Yep, we're really goin' places!

An embarrassing moment
is spitting out the car window
when it's not open.

**If you don't like my driving,
then stay off the sidewalk!**

My car is so old
that it has bifocal headlights!

**Why is bumper-to-bumper
commuting time
called rush hour?**

I always buy a beat-up used car—
that way, I never have to own up
to any of the dents.

It takes a thousand nuts
and bolts to put a car together,
but only one nut
to scatter it all over the road.

A sure way to appreciate your old
car is to find out how much
a new one costs.

I have the distinct impression
that I'm diagonally parked
in a parallel universe.

It's funny how we all think we're such good drivers, yet there are still so many nuts on the road.

If a messy car is a happy car, mine is ecstatic.

King David fancied sports cars—his Triumph was heard throughout the land!

How come everyone driving faster than you is a maniac and everyone driving slower than you is a jerk?

My car has two antitheft devices—
its age and appearance.

**When everything's coming your
way, it's a sure sign that you're
driving in the wrong direction.**

I never get lost, but occasionally
I change where I want to go.

**My parents were so protective
that they put training wheels
on my tricycle.**

I took the road less traveled,
and now my car needs
a front-end alignment.

*A rainy day is a great excuse
not to wash the car.*

A bus goes twice as fast
when you're running after it
than when you're sitting in it.

*If a part breaks, you can bet it's
listed in the warranty exceptions.*

If God intended us to drive
subcompacts, He would have made
us much smaller.

That accident couldn't have been
my fault—I have no-fault insurance!

If you hesitate, you're lost—
and usually miles
from the next exit.

What an accident! I had the right of
way, but the other guy had the SUV.

My new subcompact can stop
on a dime! Then I need to get out
and push the car over it.

I wanted my teen to drive safely,
so I installed a rear view mirror
with a patrol car in it.

Fido & Fluffy

Love our furry friends!

A dog attended a flea circus
and stole the whole show.

*A dog's affection for you is in
direct proportion to how wet and
muddy he is, and how clean your
white slacks are.*

Dogs have owners; cats have staff.

*A cat never cries
over spilled milk.*

If you think you're important,
you obviously don't have a cat.

A cat has nine lives,
but a bullfrog croaks every night.

Our dog is so lazy
that he only chases parked cars.

Cats are not trainable;
humans are. And cats know this.

Anything in the house qualifies
as a cat toy or dog chew.

*I spent a year teaching my dog
how to sit. Now he's forgotten
how to stand up.*

A door is what the cat
always finds herself
on the wrong side of.

A cat is as domestic
as it chooses to be.

*My dog flunked obedience school.
He couldn't convince the teacher
that the kids ate his homework.*

My neighbor lost her dog, but she
wouldn't put up a sign at the corner.
She said that, although the dog was
smart, he couldn't read.

Barking at an empty bowl
makes food appear.

*If you want to find your cat,
just open up a book
and start reading.*

What part of meeeeeow
don't you understand?

*Cats are smarter than dogs.
After all, you can't convince eight
cats to pull a sled.*

It's not the least bit unlucky
for a black cat to cross your path,
unless you happen to be a mouse.

A dog makes friends easily
because he wags his tail instead
of his tongue.

A dog comes when called,
but a cat takes a message
and will get back to you (maybe).

My dog is really getting slow.
This morning he brought me
yesterday's newspaper.

I thought he'd be a great lapdog,
but when I got him home
and sat on his lap, he bit me.

If your dog is overweight,
you aren't getting enough exercise.

God didn't create anything
without a purpose,
but fleas come close.